Matthew Schmolle in associat
for the Finborough Theatre a
presents

CW00394144

The world premiere

SHANGRI-LA

by Amy Ng

FINBOROUGH | THEATRE

First performed at the Finborough Theatre as a staged reading as
part of *Vibrant 2014 – A Festival of Finborough Playwrights*:
Wednesday, 5 November 2014.
First performance at the Finborough Theatre: Tuesday, 12 July 2016.

SHANGRI-LA

by Amy Ng

Cast in order of appearance

Bunny Mu	**Julia Sandiford**
Nelson Wong	**Kevin Shen**
Sylvia Bass	**Rosie Thomson**
Karma Tsering	**Andrew Koji**
Hope Leahy	**Rosie Thomson**
Village Elder	**Kevin Shen**

The performance lasts approximately 75 minutes.
There will be no interval.

Director	**Charlotte Westenra**
Designer	**Yatkwan Wong**
Lighting Designer	**Hartley T A Kemp**
Composer	**Ruth Chan**
Sound Designer	**Josh Sneesby**
Stage Manager	**Rachel Middlemore**
Producer	**Matthew Schmolle**
Associate Producer	**Liz Pagett**

Cast and Creative Team

Andrew Koji | Karma Tsering

Trained at the Actors' Temple.

Theatre includes *Hidden* (Royal Court Theatre); *The Arrest of Ai Weiwei* (Hampstead Theatre); *Fu Manchu Complex* (Southwark Playhouse); *The Forgotten of The Forgotten* (Radar Festival); *In The Bar Of A Tokyo Hotel* (Charing Cross Theatre); *A Streetcar Named Desire* and *Richard III* (Actors' Temple).

Film includes *The Fast and Furious 6, Hall of Mirrors, Luck, Mercutio's Dreaming: The Killing of a Chinese Actor, Beautiful Friend, 20th Century Boys: Chapter Two – The Last Hope* and *FB: Fighting Beat*.

Television includes *Call The Midwife, The Wrong Mans, Casualty, Acquitted* and *Scrutiny*.

Julia Sandiford | Bunny Mu

Productions at the Finborough Theatre include *Sam, The Highest Jumper Of Them All*.

Trained at Royal Central School of Speech and Drama.

Theatre includes *The Woman in the Moon* (Rose Theatre, Bankside); *Stroke of Luck* (Park Theatre); *Limehouse Nights* (Kandinsky Theatre Company); *A Midsummer Night's Dream* (Southwark Playhouse); *Crazy Love* (Paines Plough); *La Dispute* (Theatre du Preau and The Theatre, Chipping Norton); *Swallow Song* (Oxford Playhouse); *The Exonerated* (Riverside Studios); *The Real Thing* (Theatre Royal Bath and National Tour); *Richard II* (Ludlow Festival) and *Myth, Propaganda and Disaster in Nazi Germany and Contemporary America* (Orange Tree Theatre, Richmond).

Television includes *Emmerdale, Tripped, Hollyoaks, Coronation Street* and *Silent Witness*.

Kevin Shen | Nelson Wong / Village Elder

Theatre includes *Yellow Face* (National Theatre and Park Theatre); *Chimerica* (Harold Pinter Theatre) and *Caught* (Arcola Theatre).

Film includes *Unlocked* and *The Rezort*.

Television includes *You, Me and The Apocalypse, Tyrant, Hoff The Record, 24: Live Another Day, Obsession: Dark Desires* and *Bite Of The Living Dead*.

Radio includes *Fear of Flying*.

Rosie Thomson | Sylvia Bass / Hope Leahy

Previous productions at the Finborough Theatre include *Fen* and *Don Juan Comes Back From The War.*

Theatre includes *The Kitchen, The Cherry Orchard* and *The Hothouse* (National Theatre); *Yes Prime Minister* (Gielgud Theatre); *I Caught Crabs in Walberswick* (Eastern Angles, Edinburgh Festival and Bush Theatre); *Starlore for Beginners and Other Plays, The Apathists Weekly Review* and *The Most Humane Way To Kill A Lobster* (Theatre503);

Stepping Out (Salisbury Playhouse); *Sleeve Notes* and *Darknet* (Southwark Playhouse); *Stinkfoot* and *The Manual Oracle* (The Yard Theatre) and *Henna Night* (Chelsea Theatre).

Film includes *Enigma* and *Women and Children.*

Television includes *Doctors, The Bill, EastEnders, Dream Team, A Touch Of Frost, Judge John Deed, Family Affairs, Second Sight* and *Love Succs (50 Ways To Kill Your Lover).*

Amy Ng | Playwright

Productions at the Finborough Theatre include *Shangri-La* as part of *Vibrant 2014 – A Festival of Finborough Playwrights,* and *Acceptance* as part of *Vibrant 2015 – A Festival of Finborough Playwrights.*

Plays include *Shoes* (Soho Theatre); *Special Occasions* (St. James Theatre and Arcola Theatre) and *A Little Night Music* (Bread and Roses Theatre and The Space).

Film includes *Prelude to a Feast.*

Book includes *National and Political Liberty* (Oxford University Press).

Charlotte Westenra | Director

Trained at University of Manchester and Donmar Warehouse.

Theatre includes *Return of The Soldier* (Jermyn Street Theatre); *Venice Preserv'd* (Spectators' Guild); *Lower Ninth* and *Kiss of the Spider Woman* (Donmar Warehouse); *Sunset Baby* (Gate Theatre); *24 Hour Plays: Celebrity Gala* (The Old Vic); *Gladiator Games* (Crucible Theatre, Sheffield); *Titanic: Scenes From the British Wreck Commissioner's Inquiry, 1912* (The Mac, Belfast) and *Brazil* and *Casablanca* (Secret Cinema).

She was recently the dramaturg on Christopher Wheeldon's *Strapless* (Royal Opera House, Covent Garden).

Her work currently in development includes *Here* by Kate Marlais and Alex Young (winner of the S+S Award) and *The Wicker Husband* by Darren Clark and Rhys Jennings (MTI Stiles and Drewe Prize).

Yatkwan Wong | Designer

Trained at the Hong Kong Academy for Performing Arts and the Royal Welsh College of Music and Drama.

Theatre includes *This Is Not a Pipe and I am Not Sherlock Holmes* (Edward Lam Dance Theatre and Hong Kong and Shanghai tour); *Circle Mirror Transformation, Attempts On Her Life, Hello Dolly* (Hong Kong Repertory Theatre); *The Wilderness* (Hong Kong Academy for Performing Arts); *God of Carnage* (Dionysus Contemporary Theatre and Hong Kong and Singapore tour), *Phaedra 2.0* (Tang Shu-wing Theatre Studio, Macau Arts Festival); *Sing High* (Macau Cultural Centre); *Shuraba* (W Theatre, Hong Kong); *Murder in San Jose* (Theatre Farmers, Macau); *Three Sisters* (Central School of Speech and Drama) and *About Bill* (Landor Theatre).

Hartley T A Kemp | Lighting Designer

Productions at the Finborough Theatre include *A Week with Tony*.

Productions with director Charlotte Westenra include *Kiss of the Spiderwoman* (Donmar Warehouse); *Lower Ninth* (Donmar Warehouse at Trafalgar Studios); *Gladiator Games* (Crucible Theatre, Sheffield) and *Sunset Baby* (Gate Theatre).

Theatre includes *Land of Our Fathers* (Theatre503, Trafalgar Studios and Wales Millennium Centre); *As Good a Time as Any* (Print Room); *Crave* and *4.48 Psychosis* (Sheffield Theatres); *A Handful of Stars* (Theatre503 and Trafalgar Studios); *Our New Girl* (Bush Theatre) and *Love, Love, Love* (Paines Plough).

Hartley has designed for productions in the West End, for the National Theatre, Royal Shakespeare Company, Donmar Warehouse, The Old Vic, Royal Court Theatre and Linbury Studio, Royal Opera House Covent Garden, and for the Almeida Theatre, BAC, Bush Theatre, Gate Theatre, Hampstead Theatre, Lyric Theatre, Hammersmith, Opera Holland Park, Menier Chocolate Factory, Southwark Playhouse, Theatre Royal Stratford East, and Tricycle Theatre. Regional Theatre includes Birmingham Rep, Bristol Old Vic, Castleward Opera, Clwyd Theatr Cymru, Northcott Theatre, Exeter, Royal Exchange Theatre, Manchester, and West Yorkshire Playhouse.

Australian theatre includes productions for Sydney Theatre Company, Belvoir Theatre, Griffin Theatre, Darlinghurst Theatre Company, Sydney Con, Siren Theatre, Ride On Theatre in New South Wales, Melbourne Theatre Company, Malthouse Theatre, Red Stitch Actors Theatre, and Little Dove Theatre Art.

European theatre includes the Gate Theatre, Dublin, English Theatre, Frankfurt, Gothenburg Opera and Tiroler Landesteater, Innsbruck. South African theatre includes *A Number* (Fugard Theatre, Cape Town). American Theatre includes *A Little Night Music* (Broadway, Off-Broadway and regional tour).

Hartley is Artistic Director of C Venues at the Edinburgh Festival.

Ruth Chan | Composer

Trained at Oxford University and the Royal College of Music for a Masters in Composition for Screen.

Theatre compositions include *Ikea the Whale* (Queen's Theatre, Barnstaple); *The Last Days of Limehouse* (Yellow Earth); *Much Ado About Nothing* (Shanghai Repertory Theatre); *Trojan Women* (Immanuel College); *There's only One Wayne Lee/Magical Chairs* (Southwark Playhouse, Beijing People's Art Experimental Theatre and Beijing International Fringe Festival) and *Pilgrimage of the Heart* (West Wing Arts Centre, Slough and Etcetera).

Film and television includes *Around China with a Movie Camera* for the British Film Institute and National Film Theatre, *A Very British Airline*, *Changing Fortunes* for BBC World, *The Trouble with Pirates* and *Attack of the Pentagon*.

Live work commissions include *Lunar Corp* (Southbank Centre/National Tour); *From the Top* (Hong Kong Art Festival); *Turandot Reimagined* (Tête à Tête Festival); *Moon's Magmatism* (Rich Mix, The Albany and Trafalgar Square); *As in a Dream* (Cambridge University Chinese Orchestra, West Road Concert Hall) and *Piccadilly Revisited* (Thames Festival, Linbury Studio, Royal Opera House Covent Garden, Hong Kong Arts Festiva; and UK Now Festival, Beijing).

Josh Sneesby | Sound Designer

Previous productions at the Finborough Theatre include *I Didn't Always Live Here*.

Trained at the University of Southampton (Saint Michael's Scholarship, Music), Producer in Residence at Sony ATV, Associate Artist with the National Youth Theatre, and Featured Artist for Periscope.

Composer/Musical Direction and Sound Designs include on *Song Night* and *Birthday* Bash (Royal Shakespeare Company); *One Man Two Guvnors* and *The Comedy of Errors* (National Theatre); *Albion* and *Little Bit Of Luck* (Bush Theatre); *Misanthropes* and *24 Hour Celebrity Gala* (The Old Vic); *Broken News* and *Molly* (Pleasance Theatre); *Closer* (Zoo Venues); *Snow Blow* (Funny Or Die); *NYT at 60* (Hatton Garden Vaults); *MG Motors Lineage* (International Tour); *Party Labour*, Shanghai Auto-Show, *The Olympics Team Welcoming Ceremony*, *Welcoming the World* (National Youth Theatre). Josh has scored and composed one-man shows *Romeo* and *Kill the Artist*; and arranged music for *Quarke* (BBC), *Still Breathing* (Shelter Point, VEVO Live Sessions) and *These Trees are Made of Blood* (Southwark Playhouse).

Rachel Middlemore | Stage Manager

Trained at Royal Central School of Speech and Drama.

Theatre includes Deputy Stage Manager for *Toast* (National Tour and 59E59 Theaters, New York City); Assistant Stage Manager for *Dinner with Friends* (Park Theatre); *When We Were Women*, *Each His Own Wilderness*, *Play-Mas*, *Little Light*, *Widower's Houses*, *Pomona* and *The Distance* (Orange Tree Theatre, Richmond) and Stage Manager for *Teddy* (Southwark Playhouse).

FINBOROUGH | THEATRE

VIBRANT **NEW WRITING** | UNIQUE **REDISCOVERIES**

'A disproportionately valuable component of the London theatre ecology. Its programme combines new writing and revivals, in selections intelligent and audacious.' *Financial Times*

'The tiny but mighty Finborough... one of the best batting averages of any London company.' Ben Brantley, *The New York Times*

'The Finborough Theatre, under the artistic direction of Neil McPherson, has been earning a place on the must-visit list with its eclectic, smartly curated slate of new works and neglected masterpieces.' *Vogue*

Founded in 1980, the multi-award-winning Finborough Theatre presents plays and music theatre, concentrated exclusively on vibrant new writing and unique rediscoveries from the nineteenth and twentieth centuries. Our programme is unique – never presenting work that has been seen anywhere in London during at least the last twenty-five years. Behind the scenes, we continue to discover and develop a new generation of theatre makers – through our literary team, and our programmes for both interns and Resident Assistant Directors.

Despite remaining completely unsubsidised, the Finborough Theatre has an unparalleled track record of attracting the finest talent who go on to become leading voices in British theatre. Under Artistic Director Neil McPherson, it has discovered some of the UK's most exciting new playwrights including Laura Wade, James Graham, Mike Bartlett, Sarah Grochala, Jack Thorne, Simon Vinnicombe, Alexandra Wood, Al Smith, Nicholas de Jongh, Dawn King, Chris Thompson and Anders Lustgarten; and directors including Blanche McIntyre.

Artists working at the theatre in the 1980s included Clive Barker, Rory Bremner, Nica Burns, Kathy Burke, Ken Campbell, Jane Horrocks and Claire Dowie. In the 1990s, the Finborough Theatre first became known for new writing including Naomi Wallace's first play *The War Boys*; Rachel Weisz in David Farr's *Neville Southall's Washbag*; four plays by Anthony Neilson including *Penetrator* and *The Censor*, both of which transferred to the Royal Court Theatre; and new plays by Richard Bean, Lucinda Coxon, David Eldridge, Tony Marchant and Mark Ravenhill. New writing development included the premieres of modern classics such as Mark Ravenhill's *Shopping and F***king*, Conor McPherson's *This Lime Tree Bower*, Naomi Wallace's *Slaughter City* and Martin McDonagh's *The Pillowman*.

Since 2000, new British plays have included Laura Wade's London debut *Young Emma*, commissioned for the Finborough Theatre; two one-woman shows by Miranda Hart; James Graham's *Albert's Boy* with Victor Spinetti; Sarah Grochala's *S27*; Peter Nichols' *Lingua Franca*, which transferred Off-Broadway; Dawn King's *Foxfinder*; and West End transfers for Joy Wilkinson's *Fair*, Nicholas de Jongh's *Plague Over England* and Jack Thorne's *Fanny and Faggot*. The late Miriam Karlin made her last stage appearance in *Many Roads to Paradise* in 2008. We have also produced our annual festival of new writing – *Vibrant – A Festival of Finborough Playwrights* annually since 2009.

UK premieres of foreign plays have included plays by Brad Fraser, Lanford Wilson, Larry Kramer, Tennessee Williams, the English premiere of Robert McLellan's Scots-language classic, *Jamie the Saxt*; and three West End transfers – Frank McGuinness' *Gates of Gold* with William Gaunt and John Bennett, Joe DiPietro's *F***ing Men* and Craig Higginson's *Dream of the Dog* with Dame Janet Suzman.

Rediscoveries of neglected work – most commissioned by the Finborough Theatre – have included the first London revivals of Rolf Hochhuth's *Soldiers* and *The Representative*; both parts of Keith Dewhurst's *Lark Rise to Candleford*; *The Women's War*, an evening of original suffragette plays; *Etta Jenks* with Clarke Peters and Daniela Nardini; Noël Coward's first play, *The Rat Trap*; Charles Wood's *Jingo* with Susannah Harker; Emlyn Williams' *Accolade*; Lennox Robinson's *Drama at Inish* with Celia Imrie and Paul O'Grady; John Van Druten's *London Wall* which transferred to St James' Theatre; and J. B. Priestley's *Cornelius* which transferred to a sell-out Off Broadway run in New York City.

Music theatre has included the new (premieres from Grant Olding, Charles Miller, Michael John LaChuisa, Adam Guettel, Andrew Lippa, Paul Scott Goodman, and Adam Gwon's *Ordinary Days* which transferred to the West End) and the old (the UK premiere of Rodgers and Hammerstein's *State Fair*, which also transferred to the West End) and the acclaimed 'Celebrating British Music Theatre' series, reviving forgotten British musicals.

The Finborough Theatre won *The Stage* Fringe Theatre of the Year Award in 2011, *London Theatre Reviews'* Empty Space Peter Brook Award in 2010 and 2012, the Empty Space Peter Brook Award's Dan Crawford Pub Theatre Award in 2005 and 2008, the Empty Space Peter Brook Mark Marvin Award in 2004, and swept the board with eight awards at the 2012 OffWestEnd Awards, including Best Artistic Director and Best Director for the second year running. *Accolade* was named Best Fringe Show of 2011 by *Time Out*. It is the only unsubsidised theatre ever to be awarded the Channel 4 Playwrights Scheme (formerly the Pearson Playwriting Award) nine times. Three bursary holders (Laura Wade, James Graham and Anders Lustgarten) have also won the Catherine Johnson Award for Pearson Best Play.

www.finboroughtheatre.co.uk

Mailing

Email admin@finboroughtheatre.co.uk or give your details to our Box Office staff to join our free email list. If you would like to be sent a free season leaflet every three months, just include your postal address and postcode.

Follow Us Online

www.facebook.com/FinboroughTheatre

www.twitter.com/finborough

Feedback

We welcome your comments, complaints and suggestions. Write to Finborough Theatre, 118 Finborough Road, London SW10 9ED or email us at admin@finboroughtheatre.co.uk

Playscripts

Many of the Finborough Theatre's plays have been published and are on sale from our website.

Finborough Theatre T-shirts

Finborough Theatre T-shirts are now on sale from the Box Office.

Friends

The Finborough Theatre is a registered charity. We receive no public funding, and rely solely on the support of our audiences. Please do consider supporting us by becoming a member of our Friends of the Finborough Theatre scheme. There are three categories of Friends, each offering a wide range of benefits.

Richard Tauber Friends – Val Bond. James Brown. Tom Erhardt. Stephen and Jennifer Harper. Bill Hornby. Richard Jackson. Mike Lewendon. John Lawson. Harry MacAuslan. Mark and Susan Nichols. Sarah Thomas. Kathryn McDowall. Barry Serjent. Lavinia Webb. Stephen Winningham.

Lionel Monckton Friends – Philip G Hooker. Martin and Wendy Kramer. Deborah Milner. Maxine and Eric Reynolds.

William Terriss Friends – Stuart Ffoulkes. Leo and Janet Liebster. Paul and Lindsay Kennedy. Corinne Rooney. Jon and NoraLee Sedmak.

Smoking is not permitted in the auditorium and the use of cameras and recording equipment is strictly prohibited.

In accordance with the requirements of the Royal Borough of Kensington and Chelsea:

1. The public may leave at the end of the performance by all doors and such doors must at that time be kept open.
2. All gangways, corridors, staircases and external passageways intended for exit shall be left entirely free from obstruction whether permanent or temporary.
3. Persons shall not be permitted to stand or sit in any of the gangways intercepting the seating or to sit in any of the other gangways.

The Finborough Theatre is licensed by the Royal Borough of Kensington and Chelsea to The Steam Industry, a registered charity and a company limited by guarantee. Registered in England and Wales no. 3448268. Registered Charity no. 1071304. Registered Office: 118 Finborough Road, London SW10 9ED. The Steam Industry is under the overall Artistic Direction of Phil Willmott. www.philwillmott.co.uk

Production Acknowledgements

The Production would like to thank Mark Rylance, Dame Judi Dench, Sir Nicholas Hytner and Sir Derek Jacobi for their support.

We would also like to thank Grosvenor Estates, Old Vic New Voices and Francois @ Parkway Studios for their support.

Many thanks to Indhu Rubasingham and Nic Wass for their dramaturgical support. Thanks too to Simon Dormandy for his helpful suggestions.

Thanks to the Orange Tree for their considerable support.

Graphic Design	**Sofi Lee Henson** and **Rebecca Pitt**
Lighting Crew	**Eren Celikdemir**, **Hakan Hafızoğlu**, **Alexis Sinchongco** and **Ozcar Martin Zagel**
Video Artist	**Ziv Chun**
Design Associate	**Natalie Pryce**
Design Associate	**Bill Ching Wo Cheung**

SHANGRI-LA

Amy Ng

Characters

BUNNY MU, *Naxi ethnic minority, tour guide for Authentic China. Twenties.*

NELSON WONG, *CEO of Authentic China, a travel agency specialising in adventure and cultural tourism 'off the beaten path' in China. Thirties.*

KARMA TSERING, *Tibetan tour operator, who is one of Authentic China's subcontractors. Thirties.*

SYLVIA BASS, *American heiress. Fifties.*

VILLAGE ELDER, *Elderly Tibetan man.*

NIMA, *Elderly Tibetan chauffeur and Living Buddha (non-speaking role).*

HOPE LEAHY, *Irish photographer. Fifties.*

Note on Doubling

The roles of Nelson and the Village Elder can be played by one actor.

The roles of Sylvia and Hope can be played by one actor.

Time

The action of the play unfolds over one week in 2014, with
flashbacks to Bunny's childhood in 2001, and a flash-forward
to 2016.

Setting

The action of the play takes place in Shangri-La, Yunnan
Province, on China's south-west border; Beijing; and
New York City.

I envision the staging to be fairly abstract – a brilliant blue sky,
and simple props (a tree, a yurt, shadows of wings to suggest
the vultures).

*This text went to press before the end of rehearsals and so may
differ slightly from the play as performed.*

Scene One

From offstage: sound of applause, the clink of champagne glasses, cocktail chatter.

Grown-up BUNNY *in Naxi costume enters. She carries a large bouquet of flowers. She looks wonderingly at Naxi children's toys scattered around the stage – a bamboo horse, straw dolls, a shuttlecock.*

She picks up the toys. She plays shuttlecock football.

GRAN'S VOICE. Bunny, have you roasted the tea leaves?

DAD'S VOICE. Bunny, have you picked the mushrooms?

GRAN'S VOICE. Bunny, have you washed the bedsheets?

DAD'S VOICE. Bunny, have you started the soup?

GRAN'S VOICE. What's going to become of you, girl.

DAD'S VOICE. Who's going to marry you.

BUNNY *finds some climbing ropes.*

GRAN'S VOICE. Don't touch those!

DAD'S VOICE. I'll whip you if you ever go up the mountain.

GRAN'S VOICE. Never go further than the lightning-struck tree.

DAD'S VOICE. The spirit paths are for men.

GRAN'S VOICE. The summit is for the spirits.

BUNNY *finds an SLR camera and a tripod lying on top of a backpack.*

Don't you dare.

DAD'S VOICE. Ever.

GRAN'S VOICE. Never.

DAD'S VOICE. Don't point that thing at me!

BUNNY *points the camera and flashes.*

Then she takes off her Naxi costume, to reveal black mountaineering gear underneath. She slings the camera and tripod around her neck. From the backpack she takes out hiking boots and a climbing harness. She puts them on. She finds a curled-up flag. She unfurls the flag which says 'Authentic China'.

BUNNY. Morning, everyone. I am Bunny Mu, your guide. This way please. Welcome to Authentic China.

Scene Two

Blackout.

NELSON (*panicked*). I can't find the rope.

BUNNY. To your left.

NELSON. I'm slipping.

BUNNY. I've got you.

NELSON. We're both slipping.

BUNNY. I won't lose you, boss.

NELSON. I can't see.

BUNNY. We're almost out of the cloud. A few more metres.

Sunlight, to reveal NELSON *and* BUNNY.

NELSON (*looks down*). A sheer cliff.

BUNNY. Hardly.

NELSON. Losing my nerve. The big four-oh coming up.

BUNNY. Don't be ridiculous.

NELSON. Not a bad way to go.

BUNNY. Don't say that.

BUNNY *sets up her tripod during* NELSON*'s ruminations.*

NELSON. It would have been such a clean way to die. My bones bleached white on the mountain. Or mummified, like the man they found in the Alps. Future archaeologists would exhume the contents of my stomach, my blackened lungs; they'll see how we've poisoned the soil, the air, the water –

BUNNY (*fixing her camera on top of the tripod*). You're being morbid.

NELSON. Something about mountains always reminds me of death.

BUNNY. Then why climb them?

NELSON. 'Because they're there.' (*Beat.*) Why do you climb mountains?

BUNNY. Sense of perspective.

BUNNY *takes a photo. She shows it to* NELSON.

NELSON. Wow. The sky's alive, the clouds little white swirls of energy, and this little dark cloud / in the bottom left –

BUNNY. That's the smog cloud around Beijing.

NELSON. Really? Brilliant. You should call it 'Cleansed'. Or 'Capital City'. I know, 'Authentic China'. (*Laughs.*) Bunny.

BUNNY. Yes?

NELSON. Before I forget…

NELSON *takes out a red packet of money.*

BUNNY (*tries to hand back the red packet*). Don't be daft.

NELSON. The worker is worthy of her wages.

BUNNY. You haven't been paying yourself a salary for months.

NELSON. Self-exploitation is one of the privileges of running your own company. But seriously – I know it's been difficult.

BUNNY. No one's blaming you for the world economy, boss.

NELSON (*clasps his hands together*). Bunny: we have a tour.

BUNNY. Great. Where?

NELSON. Shangri-La. (*Beat.*) It's for a hedge-fund multimillionaire and his wife. The wife's from money too. Chungdar's been – (*Beat.*) put away.

BUNNY. Prison?

NELSON *shakes his head*.

Mental hospital?

NELSON *nods*.

Blimey. You've got to stop taking risks.

NELSON. Don't nag.

BUNNY. What about Tiger?

NELSON. China Travel Service.

BUNNY. Another defection!

NELSON. He's got to feed his family.

BUNNY. You're too soft.

NELSON. Bunny. I'm speaking at a conference for endangered peoples.

BUNNY. Endangered *peoples*?

NELSON. Yes. Like yourself. Minorities on the verge of disappearance, you know, forces of modernity and all that.

BUNNY. We're not turtles.

NELSON. Cultural genocide. Even the Dalai Lama said it.

BUNNY. Shush!

NELSON. Oh come on, we're on a mountain, who's going to hear –

BUNNY *indicates with her head.*

NELSON *looks.*

They're miles away.

BUNNY. 'The trees have ears.'

NELSON. Just have to climb beyond the tree line then, don't we?

BUNNY. Boss!

NELSON. You're right, you're right. 'We are not at liberty to discuss politics.' Doesn't mean the old man isn't right. And sustainable tourism can reverse that trend. Everyone will be there, Bunny! WWF, UNESCO, the Nature Conservancy, the Smithsonian. The point is, there's no one to take Jim Bass – that's the hedgie – trekking around Shangri-La.

Pause.

BUNNY. You promised you'd never ask me to go back.

NELSON. We need an investor. And I know for a fact that Jim Bass is looking to give his portfolio a greener tinge.

BUNNY. I can't go back.

NELSON. Why not?

BUNNY. You know why.

NELSON. It's been twelve years.

BUNNY. Exactly. There've been too many changes on the ground since I left.

NELSON. You'll have a local tour guide as well.

BUNNY. Who?

NELSON (*beat*). Karma.

BUNNY. What??

NELSON. He knows the terrain. He owns the contacts.

BUNNY. Karma's an informer!

NELSON. You have no proof.

BUNNY. So how do you explain his mini property empire, eh? He buys up wasteland and boom, a new highway goes through it, a dam, new railtracks, and suddenly the land's worth millions.

NELSON. Maybe he just bribes Chinese officials –

BUNNY. Oh that makes it much better.

NELSON. The point is – politically, he's definitely safe. (*Holds up his hands.*) I know, too safe, but I can't afford another guide 'disappearing'.

BUNNY. You might as well start serving banana pancakes for breakfast.

NELSON. Sustainable tourism is about honour. Respect. Respecting local cultures and ecosystems. First do no harm. There's no harm in providing our clients with creature comforts –

BUNNY. So we *are* serving banana pancakes –

NELSON. We don't want to shield them from their surroundings, of course. But we do need to cushion the shock –

BUNNY. 'Cushion the shock'? There's no infrastructure in the backcountry.

NELSON. I've hired yurts.

BUNNY (*flatly*). Yurts.

NELSON. There are thousands of Mongolians there.

BUNNY. Yunnan Mongols don't live in yurts.

NELSON. I rented some from the TV studio.

BUNNY. The TV studio.

NELSON. The Genghis Khan miniseries.

BUNNY. Why don't you just check them into Hotel Shangri-La and play them slideshows of snowy mountains.

NELSON. Bunny.

BUNNY. You promised I'd never have to do this kind of tourism again.

NELSON. If I didn't have my back to the wall –

BUNNY (*beat*). If this Jim Bass does invest, will you finally get into outbound tourism?

NELSON. Yes. I have the business case all figured out. We'll target affluent Chinese who want to go off the beaten path in the West. We'll have to educate them first, of course. No spitting. No jumping queue. No speaking on mobile phones in toilets –

BUNNY. I want in.

NELSON. The Rockies, the Alps, Yellow Stone, Patagonia – just think of the photos.

Pause.

BUNNY. When?

NELSON. Monday. You're booked on the 10 a.m. flight out to Kunming.

BUNNY *takes a photo.*

Scene Three

Some days later in Yunnan province.

BUNNY *is taking photos.*

SYLVIA *enters.*

BUNNY *instantly stops taking photos and starts the stove.*

SYLVIA. This is the life! Why do we enclose our lives in villas, in penthouses; why do we inter ourselves in concrete mausoleums? I love these yurts! So close to nature, such a small carbon footprint –

BUNNY. Good morning, Mrs Bass. You like breakfast?

SYLVIA. Jim has no idea what he's missing.

BUNNY. Mr Bass come when?

SYLVIA. He's not. Apparently something urgent came up in – (*Looks at her phone; mispronounces.*) Shanxi.

BUNNY (*automatically correcting* SYLVIA*'s pronunciation*). Shanxi. He do business there?

SYLVIA. Of course he's here on business. Otherwise he'd never venture beyond Long Island – you know that poster, the world according to the New Yorker –

BUNNY. He invest in Shanxi coal mines?

SYLVIA. I really couldn't say, hun.

BUNNY. I thought he want greener portfolio –

SYLVIA. And I thought Shangri-La would. I mean – Shangri-La! Tibet! How could he not be – Anyway. His loss. Look at the dawn! I'm close to a sublime moment, I can feel it…

SYLVIA *performs sun salutation yoga.*

BUNNY *spreads a blue-and-white Tibetan door curtain on the ground for a picnic blanket.*

That's gorgeous… every stitch here a stitch in the fabric of your great tradition.

BUNNY (*in Chinese*). Authentically handmade in a Chinese factory.

SYLVIA. Please don't speak Chinese when I'm around. It makes me feel excluded… like you're keeping secrets from me. Which you don't have to –

BUNNY. Sorry, Mrs Bass.

SYLVIA. Sylvia. Please. Of course I talk to myself too – it's just one of those – habits, of solitude… must have been lonely sometimes herding yaks up in the mountains.

BUNNY. Er…

SYLVIA. Communing with nature, of course. But still. (*Glances at her phone.*) I can't believe you get 4G coverage – in the Himalayas! Maybe I could Skype with Jim.

SYLVIA *tries Skyping without success.*

She sinks down, defeated, on the Tibetan door curtain.

She takes out a Leica D-Lux camera and takes a photo.

I'll just have to show him later what he's missing then.

BUNNY (*enviously*). A Leica! Can I hold it?

SYLVIA. Sure.

SYLVIA *gives the camera off-handedly to* BUNNY, *who handles it reverently.*

SYLVIA *traces the patterns on the curtain.*

I could give these away at our – it's our thirtieth wedding anniversary next year, and I'm planning a renewal of vows. A surprise. My best friend says it resurrected their marriage… (*Beat.*) Could you get me a hundred?

BUNNY. I telephone head office and they place order.

SYLVIA. Thanks, Bunny.

SYLVIA *looks around conspiratorially, then takes out pamphlets and a photo of the Dalai Lama. She hands them to* BUNNY.

BUNNY. Thank you very much, but we are not allowed to engage in politics.

SYLVIA. But the Dalai Lama is your leader and your guide, the guardian of your threatened culture –

BUNNY. We are not at liberty to discuss politics – for your protection and ours.

SYLVIA (*enjoying her own sensationalism*). Could you go to prison for this?

BUNNY. Latte, Mrs Bass?

SYLVIA. Oh no. Yak butter tea.

BUNNY. It's very –

SYLVIA. When in Tibet, do as the Tibetans do.

    BUNNY *nods to the wings.*

    NIMA *enters, bringing tea.*

    He is wearing sunglasses, a baseball hat, and a workaday Tibetan chuba.

    SYLVIA *sips the tea and spits it out immediately, coughing.*

    During the dialogue below, NIMA *sits down, drinks the tea, then wanders off.*

BUNNY. I don't like it either. I think only Tibetans do.

SYLVIA. You're not Tibetan?

BUNNY. I am Naxi.

SYLVIA. Nazi?

BUNNY. Naxi is an ethnic minority. There are thirty-three ethnic minorities in Yunnan.

SYLVIA. Oh right, I read about that. Like Sherpas –

BUNNY. We are different.

    SYLVIA *takes out her phone.*

SYLVIA. 'Naxi is part of the Tibeto-Burman family of languages.'

BUNNY. We have a long history. Our own kingdom. Our own cities. Look! Famous explorer, Joseph Rock, he study Naxi in the thirties.

BUNNY *takes out an aged* National Geographic *magazine*.

This is my great-grandfather. Shaman.

SYLVIA *leafs through*.

SYLVIA. Fascinating! So you're from a hereditary shaman family! Are you a shaman?

BUNNY *does a short shaman dance*.

SYLVIA *cheers*.

NIMA *crosses the stage with a small hammer and collides into* BUNNY, *who falls over without finishing her dance*.

NIMA *exits*.

BUNNY. Can I get you banana pancakes, Mrs Bass?

SYLVIA. I don't do wheat.

BUNNY. Not wheat. Spelt.

SYLVIA. Dairy?

BUNNY. Soya milk.

SYLVIA. GM?

BUNNY. Organic soya beans.

SYLVIA. Chinese beans?

BUNNY. Oh no. From Brazil.

SYLVIA. Eggs?

BUNNY. Only egg whites.

NIMA *enters with a folded-up yurt in his hands*.

NIMA *starts packing away the stove*.

Nima, stop that! She hasn't even had breakfast!

NIMA *looks up at the sky and shrugs, as if to say it's late*.

SYLVIA. You know what. He's right. I can't *wait* to see / the Tiger –

BUNNY. We have a special treat today. The valley of the rhododendrons / where –

SYLVIA. Still no / Tiger Leaping Gorge?

BUNNY. I am so sorry. But there are thirty-three different types of rhododendrons in this valley. Unique in the world.

SYLVIA. You don't say. Thirty-three different kinds of rhododendrons. What is it today? Flash-flood? Collapsed bridge?

BUNNY. Avalanche.

SYLVIA. But it's May!

BUNNY. It's the Himalayas.

SYLVIA *checks the weather on her phone and sighs in frustration as the avalanche is confirmed*.

SYLVIA. Can't believe they roll out 4G coverage for three nomads and their yaks.

KARMA *enters, in full nomadic regalia*.

KARMA. Telecommunications are controlled by the Chinese military. Who are not restricted by commercial considerations, of course. We are caught, like flies, in their spider's web.

BUNNY (*in Chinese*). No politics!

KARMA. Tashi Delek. Tashi Delek. That's 'top of the morning to you' in Tibetan. (*Bows deeply*.) I'm your guide, Karma.

SYLVIA. As in fate.

KARMA (*beams*). Exactly. I see you are a lady of wisdom. Most people think it's Karma as in Kama Sutra. (*Solemnly*.) I'm so sorry for the delay in joining you, dear lady. One of my orphanages burnt down in Diqing.

SYLVIA. You run orphanages?

KARMA. Yes, ma'am. For Tibetan children whose parents have been imprisoned by the Chinese authorities.

BUNNY (*in Chinese*). Are you out of your mind?

KARMA (*in Chinese*). Pah. This is just tourist small talk.

BUNNY (*in Chinese*). I'm not going to jail for your small talk.

SYLVIA. That's terrible.

KARMA (*in Chinese*). Who's going to know? Or are you an informer? (*In English.*) They want to destroy us. But we Tibetans must keep the flame burning.

BUNNY (*in Chinese*). Me? Hah! The whole world knows you're the informer.

KARMA. My foundation runs orphanages and schools, supports monasteries, restores temples and religious art to keep our spiritual tradition alive. With the help of our generous foreign sympathisers, of course. (*Bows.*)

BUNNY (*in Chinese*). You don't waste any time, do you?

SYLVIA. That's wonderful. Can't they just get snowploughs to –

KARMA. Alas, we are a backward country.

SYLVIA. They blew rain clouds away during the Olympics.

KARMA. I think it suits the Chinese to keep us Tibetans snow-bound.

SYLVIA. Such injustice! But, Karma, I haven't had my sublime moment – I can't wait much longer – my son's graduating from Harvard in a week! Rhododendrons aren't going to do it –

KARMA. The Tiger Leaping Gorge is gorgeous. But you have your Grand Canyon, as so many of your fellow countrymen have pointed out. We're going for bigger stakes here. This is a journey into enchantment. Bye bye, Kansas. We're venturing into valleys of psychedelic flowers, forests of magic mushrooms, where shamans brew their potions to see visions –

BUNNY (*in Chinese*). What a load of –

KARMA. Rare species, on the brink of extinction, never before seen by Western eyes. Snow leopards. Golden monkeys, glittering between the branches.

SYLVIA. We've seen the monkeys.

Vultures in the distance.

Vultures!

KARMA. They feed off yaks.

BUNNY. We are close to a sky burial site.

KARMA (*loudly*). Yaks are so stupid. They fall off cliffs –

SYLVIA. What's a sky burial?

BUNNY. Where Tibetans lay out their dead for the vultures.

KARMA *puts his arm around* SYLVIA*'s shoulders.*

KARMA. And did I mention the land of the Mosuo women, a land with no fathers and no husbands –

SYLVIA. Is that the land of the matriarchs mentioned in the Dalai Lama's tracts?

KARMA. The very same.

SYLVIA. To think they still exist!

KARMA. Confident, powerful, graceful women. They play with their toyboys, sure, but at the end of the day, they own the land, they control the money, they make the decisions. There is no jealousy, no male domination, no violence. There is peace. Shangri-La. (*Makes an expansive gesture with his arms.*) So what are we waiting for? Carpe diem!

Ushers SYLVIA *towards the car offstage.*

(*In Chinese.*) Not another word about sky burials.

BUNNY (*in Chinese*). What's the big deal? It's even in *Lonely Planet.*

KARMA. She'll want to see one next! I know them. So shut your cunt mouth. Little girls should be seen but not heard.

Scene Four

2001.

BUNNY *is fourteen years old. She is wearing Naxi costume and enters the room with a big pile of laundry and some tiffin carriers. Her English is more rudimentary than in her adult scenes.*

Two analogue SLR cameras, a compact digital camera, and a tripod and monopod lie on the bed. BUNNY *glances furtively around, then examines the digital camera. She turns it on. She examines the screen at the back of the camera with great interest, but is confused that it displays a photo of a rock.*

HOPE *enters.* BUNNY *is so engrossed she doesn't notice.* HOPE *watches for a while.*

HOPE. You need to switch it back to live view.

BUNNY. Sorry! I bring picnic lunch and – sorry!

HOPE. It's okay.

BUNNY. Sorry! No tell Father okay?

HOPE. It's cool. We're cool. I'd be curious too.

BUNNY. This camera different.

HOPE. It's a digital camera. New technology. You can take hundreds of photos without ever developing film. I use it to check lighting, framing, before the final shoot on one of the SLRs.

HOPE *takes a photo, and shows it to* BUNNY.

See? It displays instantly.

BUNNY *takes the camera and scrolls tentatively through the pictures.*

BUNNY. You take twenty photos of rock. But light different.

HOPE. I was experimenting with different filters. You can do this with digital photography.

BUNNY. Here you put rock in the middle, there you put rock at the side.

HOPE. Framing. That's the alpha and omega of photography. Go ahead. You try.

BUNNY. I have work.

BUNNY *starts pulling the bedsheets off the bed*.

HOPE. How old are you?

BUNNY. Fourteen.

HOPE. Child labour. Girl-child labour. Your brother's playing outside. Go on. You can spare five minutes.

HOPE *hands over her camera to* BUNNY.

Wait. Think of the framing. What do you want in the shot? Where do you want it?

BUNNY *considers, then takes her first picture*.

HOPE *looks critically at* BUNNY*'s photo*.

Not bad. Why did you choose to foreground this blanket?

BUNNY. My grandmother's.

HOPE. Try it with a longer exposure. That's how you adjust for exposure – see? You will have to keep very still.

BUNNY *tries again. They examine the result together.*

BUNNY. The colours…

HOPE. Yes. You have a good eye. Granny's dead, isn't she?

BUNNY. How did you –

HOPE. Because the whole tone of your photo is commemorative. You loved her very much.

BUNNY *nods*.

HOPE *takes a picture of* BUNNY.

BUNNY (*by rote*). One dollar for a portrait in traditional Naxi festival costume; five dollars for me and my brother dancing; twenty dollars for my father in shaman robes.

HOPE. Forget it.

BUNNY. You angry?

HOPE. It's degrading.

BUNNY. Why?

HOPE. Because it's cheap and – it makes you a commodity! It's not real! I haven't travelled halfway around the world to take photos of a fake shaman.

BUNNY. But my father is real – look!

BUNNY *takes out an old* National Geographic *magazine.*

This is my great-grandfather. A famous white man lived here for long time, took photos –

HOPE. Yeah yeah I know. Joseph Rock. You Naxi have been dining out on him ever since.

BUNNY. My father is the seventeenth hereditary shaman of the Mu tribe.

HOPE. Did the other sixteen run hotels?

BUNNY. Communists banned shamans.

HOPE. Alright, cool your jets. (*Beat.*) Can you prove your father is a real shaman?

BUNNY. Everybody know.

HOPE. Do you have documentary proof?

BUNNY (*holding up magazine*). This my great-grandfather.

HOPE. That could be anyone.

BUNNY. Ask any Naxi on street.

HOPE. If your father were a real shaman, wouldn't he be performing rites at the Spirit House?

BUNNY. When people need, yes.

HOPE. Take me there.

BUNNY. It taboo!

HOPE. Listen to me. I've been coming here for years. Before all this 'Shangri-La' nonsense, when it was still a perfectly pleasant little town called Zhongdian. Why you people would even want to rename your hometown after a Frank Capra movie – you don't see New Zealand calling itself Middle Earth, do you? This is by far the cleanest hostel with the best banana pancakes, but you're always half-empty. Unlike those fleabag Tibetan establishments down the road. Let's face it, Tibetan sells better. Where's your Dalai Lama? Your Richard Gere? The only reason why you even get a mention in travel books is because some white explorer photographed you seventy years ago. But if I took photos of a Naxi shaman performing his rites – I could put you on the map again.

BUNNY. Even I never be in Spirit House.

HOPE. How come?

BUNNY. I girl.

HOPE. That's ridiculous. Many cultures hold female shamans in honour.

BUNNY. It taboo.

HOPE. I know you're scared of him. He is scary. He was really quite crazed last night –

BUNNY. He was full of the spirit –

HOPE. Full of liquid spirits, certainly. I promise. He'll never know. Look at this tele-lens. I can take photos from half a mile away.

BUNNY. It taboo.

HOPE *sighs in exasperation, then starts packing her photo bag.*

HOPE. Do you know anyone getting married or with a big birthday coming up?

BUNNY. My cousin...

HOPE. I'm happy to take photos for free – look.

HOPE *shows* BUNNY *a portfolio.*

BUNNY. This paper beautiful. These colours...

HOPE. Royal Kodak paper. I wouldn't use your local photo paper to wipe my ass.

BUNNY. Why you do?

HOPE. Access. Twenty beautiful prints of you all lined up like this – (*Grins madly, flashes 'V' sign.*) And I get some candids. Degas moments, I call them. He painted ballerinas backstage. Unglamorous. Exhausted.

BUNNY. What you do with photos?

HOPE. Sell them.

BUNNY. Who buy?

HOPE. Magazines. Art galleries if I ever make it. Collectors. When's your cousin's wedding?

BUNNY. Not wedding. Naming ceremony for son.

HOPE. Good. I don't have any of those.

BUNNY. Next week.

HOPE. I can wait a week.

BUNNY. She not like you sell photos to other ghost people.

HOPE. You don't have to tell her, do you?

BUNNY *turns to leave.*

I'm not a voyeur. I'm doing a photo essay on the tribal women of Shangri-La. I've taken photos of Bai women, Dai women, and I'm really hoping to gain access to the Mosuo. I know about small oppressed nationalities. I'm Irish. My mission is to give voice to the voiceless.

BUNNY. Give them camera.

HOPE *takes out a cheap disposable camera.*

HOPE. I've given these out all over Yunnan.

BUNNY. Give them good camera.

HOPE. Who do you think I am? Father Christmas? I work for my living I'll have you know. Or do you think all white people are rich? You know how many shitty wedding gigs it took to buy these few weeks of freedom / out here?

BUNNY. You sell shaman rites photo so much money.

HOPE (*beat*). Perhaps.

BUNNY. Give me that.

Pause.

HOPE *hands* BUNNY *the digital camera.*

The Amethyst Dragon mountain. Climb north face till you reach lightning-struck tree. The Spirit House lies beyond the tree.

Scene Five

Strings of Tibetan prayer flags against the sky.

A stream.

KARMA *is busy fishing out closed lotus buds from the stream, and replacing them with open lotus flowers.*

BUNNY. That's a new low, even for you. Dressing up the chauffeur as a Living Buddha –

KARMA. Are you going to make yourself useful?

BUNNY. Seriously. Lotus flowers, at this altitude? Even *she* would smell a rat –

KARMA. They never do.

    KARMA *starts peeling the petals off the buds.*

BUNNY. This is Nelson's trip, Nelson promised her
    authenticity, I won't have you stink up Nelson's good name
    – (*Beat.*) I'm going to tell her.

KARMA. They come with their flickering scared dead eyes.
    They've tried everything else. I give them a reason to go on
    living. You want to take that away from her?

    SYLVIA *enters. A white Tibetan prayer scarf hangs loosely*
    around her shoulders.

SYLVIA. That was – oh my God – that was so – I tell you – what
    spiritual power. It was so good of His Holiness to see us.

    KARMA *scatters lotus petals over* SYLVIA *who squeals*
    with delight.

KARMA. We were very lucky. His Holiness only meditates
    outside his cave every three months.

SYLVIA. Such nobility in his face.

KARMA. Close your eyes. Yes. Let the encounter sink into the
    depths of your soul –

    KARMA *puts both hands on each side of* SYLVIA*'s head.*

    …like the reverberations of a temple gong… a summons
    from another world.

SYLVIA. Oh I so wish he had opened his eyes and gazed into
    mine…

KARMA. Sylvia, Sylvia, do you know how rare it is to glimpse
    a Living Buddha in deepest meditation?

SYLVIA. I know, Karma. Absolutely. I am so aware of the
    privilege… I just want to lay bare my heart to him, to be
    seen and to be grasped and to be understood, to have him
    look into my eyes – to be revealed to him…

KARMA (*half-jokingly*). Be careful what you wish for, Sylvia.
    (*Puts his hands over* SYLVIA*'s eyes.*) Breathe in, white,

spirituality; breathe out, black, fear, anger... a person before Enlightenment is like a closed lotus bud, but you, Sylvia, are a lotus blossom opening towards the light.

KARMA *steers* SYLVIA *to the stream.*

Open your eyes.

SYLVIA. How gorgeous.

KARMA. That's you. That's your soul. When we came the buds were closed tight. And now look at them!

NIMA *enters, dressed as usual in his worn-out Chuba and sunglasses.*

BUNNY. Look. There's Nima.

SYLVIA. Who?

BUNNY. Our driver. Where have you been all morning, Nima? (*Whipping out her camera.*) Stand right there, Nima. The light reflects so wonderfully on the nobility of your features.

KARMA (*in Chinese, hissing*). What do you think you're doing.

BUNNY (*to* SYLVIA). The play of light around his face, like an aura, right, Mrs Bass?

KARMA (*in Chinese*). They only see what they want to see.

SYLVIA. I'm not really a photographer, dear. I just want to keep a record of my journey on earth... I won't deny I was much photographed in my salad days –

KARMA. You are the most beautiful subject a photographer could desire.

SYLVIA. That was the springtime of my life... but now my days are in the yellow leaf.

KARMA. What are you talking about? I have seen your sprightly, spring-like aura.

BUNNY (*in Chinese, holding up her camera*). What if I show the woman these two photos?

KARMA (*in Chinese*). The Buddha can appear as a king, a leper, a prostitute, why not a chauffeur?

BUNNY (*in Chinese*). Pleeee-aaa-se. I'm not one of your gullible clients.

KARMA (*in Chinese*). How do you know Nima's not a Living Buddha?

SYLVIA. Excuse me, you two. English.

KARMA (*in Chinese, takes out a photo*). Do you remember the Living Buddha in the Simbiling monastery? Look closely at Nima's face.

Vultures.

SYLVIA. Vultures! So close! I need my camera.

SYLVIA *exits.*

KARMA (*in Chinese*). Do you remember the raid? A month after those three monks set themselves on fire? I knew they'd attack after the footage went viral. I got to the Living Buddha just in time, two hours before the police, disguising him as my chaffeur to get through military checkpoints. Nima is the Living Buddha.

Scene Six

2001.

A lightning-struck tree stage-right.

Fourteen-year-old BUNNY *practises taking photos with her newly acquired digital camera.*

HOPE *enters. She watches* BUNNY *for a while.*

HOPE. How are you getting on? Let's take a look.

BUNNY *clutches the camera.*

Don't worry. A deal's a deal. I'm not going to take it back.

BUNNY *shows her the photos on the camera display screen.*

HOPE *scrutinises the photos intently.*

This is *worlds* better… You're a natural. This photo. Try it
again. But with flash.

She programmes the camera to flash and hands it back to
BUNNY, *who shoots.*

They look at the result together.

BUNNY (*critically*). The colours are strange.

HOPE. You've got the white balance wrong. The light's
deceptive. It seems warm but actually it's very bleaching.

BUNNY *takes another picture. They examine it together.*

BUNNY (*whispers*). Wow.

HOPE. That's what we do. We paint with light. (*Looks through
the lenses.*) I tell you what. Try taking the same photo again,
but from a higher elevation.

HOPE *returns the camera to* BUNNY, *then advances
beyond the lightning-struck tree.*

BUNNY. Female can't go there!

HOPE. Nonsense. I've been up here a whole week, and your
mountain gods haven't struck me dead.

BUNNY. You foreigner. I cannot.

HOPE. Of course you can.

BUNNY. No!

HOPE *swoops down on* BUNNY *and takes away the camera.*

HOPE. You don't deserve this camera.

BUNNY. We make deal! Give me back!

HOPE. If you're serious about photography, you must be
prepared to break taboos.

BUNNY. Why?

HOPE. A real photographer will go to any lengths to take pictures that are truthful. And the path to truth involves breaking taboos. Look at Nan Goldin and Robert Mapplethorpe, breaking every taboo around sex; look at Lee Miller! They brought more light into the world; their courage still enlarges.

BUNNY. I don't understand.

HOPE. I think you do. You wanted that camera so much you were prepared to betray your father's whereabouts to me. That told me you had the potential to be a real artist. I could have been wrong. Maybe you did it just for an expensive camera.

BUNNY. No!

HOPE. Then prove it. Walk across the line.

HOPE *walks beyond the lightning-struck tree and waves the camera at* BUNNY.

BUNNY. That not fair!

HOPE. That photo, of the shadow of this mountain slicing the opposite peak. It was a good photo. But it could be a great photo. From higher up, you can look down on that peak. And you can see vultures, circling that peak, half of them gleaming gold in the sun, the other half plunged in darkness. Would you cross the line for the perfect photo?

BUNNY *tries taking a few steps towards the lightning-struck tree.*

BUNNY. I can't.

HOPE *throws* BUNNY *a cheap disposable camera.*

HOPE. Look at this tree through your lens. How would you frame it? Would you emphasise the verticality of the trunk, or the diagonal of the branch?

BUNNY *looks through the lens, adjusts. Takes a shot.*

What about from slightly closer? How does the tree change?

BUNNY *takes a step and takes another shot.*

What about a close-up?

BUNNY *takes another step. She is right next to the tree.*

How would the tree look from the other side? Look how the branch loses its angularity, how rounded it looks now. How would you convey that change in feeling?

BUNNY, *looking through the lens, crosses the line.*

HOPE *grips* BUNNY.

You did it!

BUNNY *lowers the camera, dazed.*

Whenever you're afraid, whatever you don't understand, even if the world collapses around you – make it into art.

HOPE *ceremonially hangs the digital camera around* BUNNY*'s neck.*

The sound of shamanistic drums.

BUNNY. That's –

HOPE. Come on. There's a bush on a ledge overlooking the Spirit House. I've been holed up there a week.

BUNNY. Why?

HOPE. To take photos of Dear Old Dad, of course.

BUNNY. You dare?

HOPE. Here I stand. Unscathed.

BUNNY (*fiercely*). You no let anyone see photos of my father. I forbid!

HOPE. You forbid? (*Laughs.*) I like you. You're feisty. You're not going to end your days slaving for your man, an old woman by age thirty –

BUNNY. Give me film!

HOPE. If you take a photo of your dad, I'll give you the film. Deal? I don't mind admitting – I just couldn't seem to frame it correctly. But you – you have an amazing eye. You can do justice to your dad.

BUNNY. Taboo taboo taboo! Spirits will strike dead –

HOPE. I don't believe in gods or ghosts. But I do believe that our conscience keeps the score. If you sell out your own taboos for gain, you let loose the demons in your mind. I've broken many taboos. But always in pursuit of art. And here I stand. So the question is: what sort of person are you? Are you the kind who will sell their father's secrets for an expensive camera?

BUNNY. No!

HOPE. So you have a duty to share this with the world, you know.

BUNNY. Shaman rites only for Naxi.

HOPE. Oh come on. Only tourists need shamans nowadays. Your father's one of the last, isn't he? Who's going to be his heir? Your brother?

BUNNY. He don't want to learn. Too hard work.

HOPE. The seventeenth hereditary shaman, the last of his kind, using his body to paint the symbols of the only living hieroglyphic language in the world. And all this will be lost in time, unless you capture it with your lenses.

Pause.

HOPE *heads off towards the Spirit House.*

She looks back at BUNNY.

BUNNY *follows.*

The sound of intense drumming.

BUNNY *returns, with torn-out film in her hands, cupping her digital camera as if it were a treasure, staring at the image of her dad on her screen.*

Scene Seven

KARMA *and* SYLVIA *are meditating.*

KARMA *hits the side of a meditation bowl, which chimes.*

KARMA. How did that feel?

SYLVIA. My monkey brain kept on chattering away. I just couldn't push away the thoughts.

KARMA. Don't push them away. Be mindful. Observe them.

SYLVIA (*restlessly*). I just can't.

Vultures.

They sound hungry today.

KARMA (*loudly*). Are you hungry?

KARMA *takes out some cheese from his bag.*

Try this.

SYLVIA *tries it, somewhat gingerly, then with increasing enthusiasm.*

SYLVIA. Yum… like Camembert… but better.

KARMA. I got French experts to work with our local yak-butter producers – all organic, of course, free-range yak, part of my ongoing efforts to lift Shangri-La Tibetans out of poverty, sustainably… look at this!

KARMA *pulls out a bottle of red wine and two wine glasses.*

SYLVIA. The Shangri-La Red Wine Company? Cabernet Sauvignon no less.

KARMA. Yes. I spotted the opportunity – all our warm riverbeds, our steep sunny slopes…

KARMA *pours out wine for himself and* SYLVIA.

SYLVIA (*laughs*). I can't believe I'm having wine and cheese with a Tibetan nomad in the Himalayas.

KARMA. Why not? It's good, isn't it?

SYLVIA. Very good.

KARMA. If we only had investment – we could roll this out throughout the region, rescue thousands of villages from poverty and dependency on the Chinese –

SYLVIA. What's a man like you doing, working for a Chinese travel company?

KARMA. I don't think of it as working for the Chinese. I have a fantastic job. I get to introduce foreigners to our culture.

SYLVIA. Oh Karma, Karma, if you had Nelson's advantages – Harvard Business School. Oxford. Goldman Sachs.

KARMA. I am a Tibetan nomad. He's the son of a rich Hong Kong family. Our karmas have ripened differently.

SYLVIA. You provide all the labour, and he takes the kudos.

KARMA. In eight years he's really built the 'Authentic China' brand. It's synonymous with sustainable tourism in China.

SYLVIA. You're the real thing. A genuine Tibetan nomad. The least he could do is make you partner.

KARMA. He won't. I asked.

SYLVIA. Chinese-Tibetan relations for you in a nutshell!

KARMA. But my clients come to me direct the second time. And the third time. Authentic China used to be one hundred per cent of my business. Now it's seventy-five per cent. My goal is fifty per cent. That's what I wanted from Nelson in the beginning. Fifty-fifty.

The sound and shadows of vulture wings (think soundtrack of Hitchcock's The Birds).

KARMA *curses violently, with real animosity, in Tibetan, and throws rocks at the vultures.*

Profound silence.

SYLVIA. You're okay? You're shaking.

KARMA. It's cold.

SYLVIA. I thought you Tibetans revered vultures as – 'sky dancers'?

KARMA. They're filthy creatures!

SYLVIA. Why? Don't they perform a necessary function.

KARMA. We should get back to meditation.

SYLVIA *wraps her white scarf around* KARMA.

SYLVIA (*flirtatiously*). You know what kind of meditation I've been dying to try out?

KARMA. Tantric?

SYLVIA. How did you know?

KARMA. Just a guess.

SYLVIA. You must be inundated with women clamouring for lessons in tantric meditation.

KARMA. Tantric meditation is the secret heart of Buddhism. For a man to contact his inner woman, and a woman to contact her inner man.

SYLVIA. That's so Jungian!

KARMA. There is a secret valley – a monastery dug out of the mountainside – cave after cave of sacred art, manuscripts. What Tantric secrets slumber in those caves! So much, so much was destroyed during the Cultural Revolution. I've heard there are scientists in the West who can restore burnt manuscripts with ultrasound. Ten million dollars and this heritage could be secured for the whole world.

SYLVIA. If only Jim – I'm worried, Karma! He's become... so bored. Jim lives his life like he runs his hedge funds – hedged against all risks...

KARMA. What a compassionate soul you are, Sylvia. Yes, Jim must be suffering greatly. We must think of a way to help him.

KARMA *pushes both hands against* SYLVIA*'s.*

For this meditation we need skin to skin contact.

KARMA *starts taking off his chuba.*

SYLVIA. I want to do this with my husband.

KARMA. Of course. Let me show you how.

KARMA *tries to unbutton* SYLVIA*'s blouse.*

SYLVIA *pushes him away.*

SYLVIA. I can't – I'm sorry if I've – stop, Karma!

KARMA *flings himself down in front of* SYLVIA*'s feet.*

KARMA. Sylvia! You're a queen amongst women. A Bodhisattva of compassion! Who refuses to enter the heaven of nirvana herself before every sentient being is rescued from their suffering!

SYLVIA. There's never been anyone but Jim.

Scene Eight

SYLVIA *scrolls through her images on her camera.* BUNNY *hovers next to her.*

BUNNY. Nelson is dominant player in sustainable tourism in China.

SYLVIA. Every photo looks so flat.

BUNNY. You need flash.

SYLVIA. But it's so bright.

BUNNY. Therefore flash. Common beginners' mistake, to use flash only in dark. This light is draining. Nelson is at the Conference of Endangered Peoples right now, talking to British Museum, Nature Conservancy, Greenpeace. Maybe he runs their tours for them.

SYLVIA. Good for him. (*Beat.*) It's not the flash. Don't get me wrong. It's gorgeous here. But the sublime – the sublime moment – maybe in the land of the matriarchs. Karma says we're going today to a Mosuo village!

BUNNY. Which one?

SYLVIA. He didn't say.

BUNNY. Close or far?

SYLVIA. Only half an hour away.

BUNNY. Oh.

Vultures.

SYLVIA. The vultures fly along a straight line perpendicular to us. Are the sky burial sites located along meridian lines or something?

BUNNY. They fly along the new highway. Roadkill.

SYLVIA. Oh. People too?

BUNNY. Many builders killed, and villagers – they do not understand that cars go so fast. Nelson only needs a one-off investment to roll out operations throughout Asia. And I know Mr Bass need more green companies for portfolio.

SYLVIA. Then send him a proposal.

BUNNY. I know you have family foundation. You can fund Nelson.

SYLVIA. Oh you know that, do you? Perhaps if you provided an incentive…

BUNNY. I do not understand.

SYLVIA. Take me to a sky burial.

BUNNY. What?!

SYLVIA. Take us… Jim will come out for a sky burial.

BUNNY. It unthinkable!

SYLVIA. It's not unthinkable. I'm thinking it.

BUNNY. Taboo.

SYLVIA. Bunny, please! I know Karma won't – you're my only chance!

BUNNY. But why? Why?

SYLVIA. There's this extinct Native American tribe. They arranged their dead a in fetal position on a hillside, surrounded them with pebbles, then left them to the jackals. And soon there's nothing left but this outline, in the pebbles. A hundred years ago some German anthropologist made a cast of one of these outlines. It was a bid item last month at a charity auction. You'd never seen such a bidding war – not even Princess Diana's dresses – the men were like great whites – Jim won it for ten grand. And that was only the cast. Of an outline. Of a body eaten by a jackal. Whereas a sky burial...

BUNNY. You want to go sky burial – to keep husband?

SYLVIA. No! I'm not – you can't possibly – I'm not so desperate – the complexity – you really think I'm – No. No. We're going because we're each shut up in our own little bubble and neither of us feel anything and we're plastic people, we're plastic... If we were up there, on the mountains, dead, the vultures wouldn't touch us because we're pumped to the hilt with preservatives –

BUNNY (*confused*). But you only eat organic.

SYLVIA. How dare you mock me, you little –

BUNNY. Sorry. I don't understand.

SYLVIA. How could you. (*Pause.*) When I first met Jim – what a pitbull. Solid. Inbuilt bullshit detector. That's why I married him. I thought 'This man is a rock. He'll never lose himself in a fairytale like my parents.' And you know what, he's never settled for counterfeits. So he fucks whores, but he knows he won't find love and happiness with some augmented blonde twenty-two-year-old. He has his Ferrari and his Maserati but he knows it won't make him young again. So when I saw him so – transfigured – is that the word? – by this cast, of this corpse, eaten by jackals, I thought that's it. There's nothing more real than death. It's the only thing that can resurrect us.

BUNNY. You have your own money. You do not need man.

SYLVIA. I met Jim at eighteen. Daddy's right-hand man. And he singled me out. The boss's daughter. I dropped out of college to marry him. This is all I know.

BUNNY. But you can learn –

SYLVIA. Okay okay I admit it. I'm pathetic. But you'd do anything for your Nelson too, wouldn't you? You just have to show me the way, take me to the rock and wait for me –

BUNNY. It's against everything Nelson stands for – honour, respect for tradition, boundaries –

SYLVIA. How is it disrespecting the Tibetans if we watch a sky burial? Isn't it a kind of – worship – really, a spiritual test, a lesson, in the impermanence of life, the reality of death –

BUNNY. Lady, it is wrong!

Pause.

SYLVIA (*coldly*). I'm afraid my family foundation gets thousands of worthy proposals every year. We're overextended already. I see no reason to fund a Chinese company profiting from Tibetans.

BUNNY. Then at least no money to Karma.

SYLVIA. Karma has not asked for a single – he doesn't even know / about my –

BUNNY. Of course Karma know! His Shangri-La Red Wine Company big investor is Chinese government. He bribe Beijing. He get money from American and European NGOs. This Mosuo village he want to take you to – fake. Tourists think Mosuo women free love, free sex, but Mosuo don't like sex tourists. This fake village import Thai dancers and prostitutes / from across –

SYLVIA (*angrily*). I don't believe a word! Karma is too respectful of women / to ever –

BUNNY. Do you want proof?

Pause.

SYLVIA. No.

BUNNY (*beat*). I'm sorry.

SYLVIA *exits, head held high, trying not to cry.*

KARMA *enters from the other side and twists* BUNNY*'s arm behind her back.*

KARMA. You'll regret this.

BUNNY. I'm the tour leader. You're just the subcontractor. I represent Nelson here.

KARMA. The mountains are high, Nelson is far away.

BUNNY. I know what you're up to. I'll tell Nelson.

KARMA. And I'll tell him you're planning to take clients to watch a sky burial. Guess how your precious Nelson will react / to that –

BUNNY. I've just said no and no and no! I know you lost most of your capital in that golf course because someone in Beijing finally noticed it was in a national park! You need Nelson's business, his rich white clients. And if Nelson finds out about that golf course...

KARMA *releases her.*

KARMA. You idiot. All these years Nelson's held you back. You could have flown the ghetto, made something of your life –

BUNNY. Nelson gave me meaning and purpose –

KARMA. Sustainable tourism is a trap!

BUNNY. A second lease on life!

KARMA. Keep us poor, make us stay on the land. Display us like safari wildlife to rich white –

SYLVIA (*offstage*). Karma!

KARMA. You're even more pathetic than her. In love with your own jailer... (*In English.*) Coming, my Bodhisattva!

KARMA *exits.*

Scene Nine

2003.

The backpacker's hostel in Shangri-La.

Sixteen-year-old BUNNY *hammers netting into place in the courtyard, sealing it up to form a cage. She has a Nikon F4 SLR camera around her neck.*

NELSON *enters, holding a recent issue of the* National Geographic.

NELSON. Is this the hostel of the seventeenth hereditary shaman of the Mu–

BUNNY. Put away that magazine immediately.

NELSON. But it features the shaman performing his rites –

BUNNY. Out of my sight. Please.

   NELSON *stuffs the magazine into his backpack.*

NELSON. But this is the hostel owned by the shaman?

BUNNY. I cannot have that magazine under our roof.

   NELSON *throws the magazine into the wings.*

NELSON. Better?

   BUNNY *nods, relieved.*

Do you have a room for the week?

BUNNY. I'm sorry. We're completely booked.

NELSON. Oh. How disappointing. I studied anthropology in college – Joseph Rock – oh look, there. (*Points at a framed photo of the ageing* National Geographic *from the thirties.*)

BUNNY. That's my great-grandfather.

NELSON. So you're the shaman's daughter.

BUNNY. Yes. You could try the Tibetan hostel next door.

   BUNNY *works on her nets.*

NELSON. What are you doing?

BUNNY. We need to – secure the courtyard. My brother got the cheapest possible bird netting which developed a hole. This is much better quality –

NELSON. Are you keeping rare butterflies? Birds?

BUNNY *doesn't answer and continues to work on the nets.*

A commotion.

Screaming.

What's that?

BUNNY. Everything's fine.

NELSON *cranes to see what's going on.*

BUNNY *tries to block his view.*

NELSON. That's the shaman!

BUNNY. He's not well.

NELSON. They've tied him up!

BUNNY. He's possessed by the spirits. He needs to be kept safe.

NELSON. Is that what the netting's –

BUNNY. To keep him safe!

NELSON. Is he – dangerous?

BUNNY. No, no, you're perfectly safe. We just need to stop him escaping.

NELSON. But if he's not dangerous / why –

BUNNY. Because the neighbours don't – the boys throw stones – they think he's cursed.

NELSON. Why?

BUNNY. Tourists like you! Waltzing in with that magazine!

NELSON. What's wrong with the magazine? Have you even seen these photos? Your father looks sublime, the expression on his face – transfigured with light –

BUNNY. It's taboo taboo taboo –

NELSON. What's taboo?

BUNNY. The rites! Witnessing the rites in the Spirit House!
They're secret! When Father saw his photograph he went –

Pause.

NELSON. Let me get this straight. These rites, the Spirit House,
are taboo for outsiders. This photograph was taken without
your father's permission. When he saw this photograph, he
went mad.

BUNNY. Yes.

NELSON. That's abhorrent. How could anyone do that – as if
you were wild animals, through a tele-lens. You should sue
this photographer this –

NELSON *goes offstage and comes back with the* National
Geographic. *He peers at it.*

Hope Leahy.

BUNNY. Get rid of it!

NELSON. No. You've got to face this. What's your name?

BUNNY. Bunny.

NELSON. Make a stand, Bunny. Leave this with me. I have a
law background. I'll find her agent, / send her –

BUNNY. No! I just want to move on!

NELSON. She probably made a lot of money out of these
photos. Didn't think someone who could take such photos –
I mean, the sheer glory and the power – just goes to show.
I'll sue her for damages – emotional distress, psychological
harm, the lot.

BUNNY. No, I beg you – don't make things worse.

NELSON. If you were in Europe, she would have had to ask
your permission – I take it she didn't.

BUNNY. No.

BUNNY *cries*.

NELSON. Listen. We've got to fight back. You're not animals in a safari. You're a people with its own customs, history, tradition, as deserving of respect and care as any other people on earth.

BUNNY*'s father screams*.

BUNNY. I've got to go. Don't contact the photographer.

NELSON. I won't without your permission. But do think about it. I'm sure I can get my friends to work on your case pro bono. Here's my card.

Scene Ten

Blackout.

BUNNY (*in Chinese*). This better be worth it.

Sound of someone falling.

SYLVIA *screams*.

KARMA. I'm sorry. The only access is through this natural tunnel. It's why this village alone survived war and conquest throughout the centuries. The whole village is a monastery, hewn out of a rock face. Holy, holy, holy. Lhasa may be the public face, but this is the hidden heart of Tibet. Take off your shoes. You are treading on sacred ground.

BUNNY (*in Chinese*). Don't write cheques you can't cash.

Light.

Stunned silence. It's the most beautiful sight they have ever seen.

I take back everything.

SYLVIA. Christ have mercy.

An awed BUNNY *takes out her camera and looks through the viewfinder.*

BUNNY (*softly, in Chinese*). Chinese tourist buses.

KARMA (*in Chinese*). Impossible.

BUNNY (*in Chinese*). China Travel Service.

BUNNY *hands him the camera.*

They must have built a connecting exit from the highway.

The VILLAGE ELDER *comes running out.*

ELDER. Tashi Delek. Tashi Delek. Welcome. Welcome.

KARMA (*in Tibetan*). I paid for exclusive access, old man.

ELDER (*in Tibetan*). Our service will not be compromised in any way.

KARMA (*in Tibetan*). We had a contract. An agreement.

ELDER (*in Tibetan*). The Chinese are leaving now. Your clients will be undisturbed this evening.

KARMA. That's not the point! Exclusivity. No more than twenty tourists a year. To protect you, this village, more than anything else –

ELDER. We don't need your protection.

SYLVIA. What is it now?

KARMA. Nothing… nothing. It appears we arrived on a bad day. There is a funeral going on for a high lama. Unfortunately we're going to have to relocate.

SYLVIA. Excuse me – sir, Bunny, can you translate?

BUNNY. My Tibetan's not so good.

SYLVIA. I would be so honoured if I were allowed to witness a sky burial.

KARMA. That's absolutely taboo.

SYLVIA. I'm willing to make donations – huge donations.

KARMA. Even the family don't stay – only the lowest caste prepares the dead for the / – it's polluting –

SYLVIA. I understand that most of the treasures of tantric meditation were destroyed during the Cultural Revolution. But there are experts in the West that can help resurrect, / I mean restore –

KARMA. There are / some things aren't for sale.

SYLVIA. I'm glad you know that, Karma.

SYLVIA *takes out a thick wad of money and presses it into the* VILLAGE ELDER*'s palms, who accepts it and intones a blessing.*

SYLVIA *points at the vultures.*

The VILLAGE ELDER *stares impassively.*

KARMA. Sylvia! They've stoned tourists trying to watch sky burials. We're leaving. Now.

KARMA *firmly ushers* SYLVIA *towards the exit.*

BUNNY. Where will we stay?

KARMA. We'll stay with the Mosuo.

SYLVIA. The real ones?

BUNNY (*in Chinese*). You're joking. It's much too primitive.

KARMA (*in Chinese*). For once, then, earn your salary! Get it up to scratch.

BUNNY (*in Chinese*). I'm the tour leader. We're staying here. The old man said the Chinese tourists are leaving. She might not even notice.

KARMA. We're leaving.

BUNNY. I'm very sorry for the inconvenience. I will order a helicopter and we will go to Shangri-La City and check in at the Sheraton.

SYLVIA. No. I want to stay in the Land of the Matriarchs. The *real* Land of the Matriarchs.

KARMA (*in Tibetan*). You'll regret this, old man.

ELDER (*in Tibetan*). This monastery was never meant to be the preserve of the rich and powerful. It is open to all.

KARMA (*in Tibetan*). Don't play the holy fool, old man. Those aren't pilgrims. They're Chinese. Mass. Tourists. How much are they paying you? *How much?*

ELDER (*in Tibetan*). The Chinese come knocking – can we say no? Ever since your father led the Red Guards through the secret tunnel, ever since they broke our statues, razed our temples, starved us, beat us, took away our lamas, have we been able to say no?

KARMA (*in Tibetan*). Not that again. My father was ten. Which ten-year-old wasn't utterly – brainwashed – during the Cultural Revolution? And I've made reparations. You come to me, you demand thousands to restore a statue. I pay. Then ten thousand, to restore a room in the monastery. I pay. Hundreds of thousands to restore an entire cave of Buddhist art. And it took a while to raise the money, I admit. But I PAID. How much did the Chinese offer?

ELDER (*in Tibetan*). They showed me title deeds. You've been buying up the land around the village. Because you knew about the highway, long before we did. You knew the land would triple in value. What do you want to do with the land? More tofu buildings?

KARMA *blanches.*

BUNNY (*in Chinese*). I knew it. I knew it.

SYLVIA. Bunny, what's the old man saying?

BUNNY. My Tibetan is not so good. But he mentioned tofu buildings.

SYLVIA. What?

BUNNY. Buildings collapse because corrupt property
    developers build cheap shoddy dangerous –

ELDER (*in Tibetan*). Schools, hospitals, children and sick
    people – dead because you cut corners and put up houses of
    cards.

KARMA (*in Tibetan*). There was an *earthquake*. Buildings
    collapse.

SYLVIA. I fail to see the relevance –

BUNNY. Shhh! I concentrate.

ELDER. Only the buildings *you* put up collapsed. Not the old
    village houses.

    *The sound of vulture wings beating, more insistent than ever
    before.*

    (*In Tibetan.*) The year of the earthquake was a very good
    year, a very good year for vultures – a bumper crop of
    unnatural human deaths.

Scene Eleven

2004.

The hostel in Shangri-La.

Seventeen-year-old BUNNY *is dressed in her father's shaman
robes. She is watching* Shaman King, *a Japanese cartoon, on
the portable VCD player. She practices a shaman dance.*

KARMA *enters, unnoticed by* BUNNY. *He takes a snapshot of*
BUNNY *dancing with the cartoon in the background.*

KARMA. So this is the famous Naxi shaman dance.

BUNNY. Who are you?

KARMA. A Tibetan.

BUNNY. So?

KARMA. Shangri-La belongs to the Tibetans.

BUNNY. No it doesn't. There've always been Naxi here.

KARMA. In Zhongdian, perhaps. But not in Shangri-La.

BUNNY. Zhongdian is Shangri-La, you idiot!

KARMA. Not any more.

BUNNY. I know who you are. You're Karma Tsering. You led the campaign to rebrand us 'Shangri-La'. They say your clan bribed the Chinese with caterpillar fungus.

KARMA. A scientifically proven aphrodisiac.

BUNNY. So that we would win…

KARMA (*in the voice of a beauty-pageant MC*). Announcing the winner of the beauty pageant – Zhongdian – from now on known as Shangri-La. (*Hands to his cheeks in shocked delight.*)

BUNNY. Your people are cowboys!

KARMA *goes around the room and casually smashes the glass frame of the old* National Geographic *photo.*

KARMA. You have forty-eight hours to close up shop. Sign this.

KARMA *thrusts a sheet of paper at* BUNNY.

BUNNY. You want to take over our nice clean hostel? Too many bedbugs in yours?

KARMA. Sign. Or I'm going to put up these photos of you learning *authentic* shaman dancing from a Japanese cartoon on TripAdvisor –

BUNNY. My father is the seventeenth hereditary shaman of the Mu clan!

KARMA *picks up the bamboo horse in the corner and snaps it in two.*

KARMA. And he's mad. Your brother's gone to the factories. You have nobody.

KARMA *rips off the straw dolls mounted on the wall and casually shreds them to pieces.*

Scene Twelve

KARMA *sits on a rock, overseeing* NIMA *digging a hole.*

A wooden toilet and folded-up yurt lie next to the hole.

KARMA. Deeper. The ghost people don't want to smell their own shit.

NIMA *fits the toilet over the hole.*

Always keep the lid down. They like hiding their shit.

NIMA *fits the yurt over the toilet.*

Tomorrow, before the first light, dig a hole... oh, next to that peach tree. Then move this whole fucking contraption there. They don't want to see yesterday's shit.

NIMA *throws down his shovel and leaves.*

Nima!

BUNNY *enters.*

BUNNY. Living Buddha deserted you?

KARMA. Get back to work!

BUNNY. I've disinfected the bedrooms. I made them take the pigs out of the houses. I've hung coils and coils of incense from every inch of the ceilings. It sort of covers the stench. I scrubbed the women's hands before cooking, and they're only using pots and pans we provide.

KARMA. And the floor?

BUNNY. We couldn't find enough clean straw to cover them.

KARMA. But they're caked with pig shit!

BUNNY. She wanted authenticity.

KARMA. Maybe we should just quarter her in the yurts for the night.

BUNNY. You think you can stop her from nosing around? She's probably handing out Dalai Lama photos right now.

KARMA. Dinner entertainment options? Folk dance, folk musicians, martial-arts display, there must be *something*.

BUNNY. The girls are pockmarked.

KARMA. Make the old women dance. We'll call it 'The Dance of the Matriarchs.' Radios? Phones?

BUNNY. Confiscated. But the Matriarch's miffed. There's some opera broadcast this evening that the whole village was going to listen to. She wants more money.

KARMA *snarls, takes out a thick stack of notes and marches offstage.*

SYLVIA *enters.*

SYLVIA. Read this.

SYLVIA *thrusts her phone at* BUNNY.

BUNNY (*reading*). 'A memorandum of intent, for Sylvia Bass, henceforth known as the investor, to purchase two million worth of shares in the Company known as "Authentic China".'

SYLVIA. This is all ready to go out to my lawyer. (*Pause.*) And I promise you Nelson won't know.

BUNNY. I can't.

SYLVIA. Are you afraid of *Karma*?

BUNNY. You will not like if I go dig up your dead relatives and watch worms eat them.

SYLVIA. You'd be welcome.

BUNNY. What?

SYLVIA. Yes. Have it all! The bouquets, the candles, the hymns, the eulogies – pillar of society, loving husband, caring father – lies lies lies lies lies. I'd much rather they'd just put out dear old dad for the vultures to eat – pick his bones clean – so clean. (*Beat.*) Are you in or out?

KARMA *enters*.

KARMA. Sylvia! I've been looking for you everywhere! The Matriarchs are ready to initiate you into the secrets / of the –

SYLVIA. I am not going.

KARMA. But, Sylvia! Something no westerner has ever seen –

SYLVIA. I'm not going! I saw a woman, she was quite young, but she opened her mouth and there were no teeth. I saw lice jumping in their hair. I saw children running around with red scraped bottoms and shit on their legs. There's nothing beautiful or regal or strong. Just poverty… filth! And they pressed in on me. They stroked my hair, my cheeks, they pulled my ear lobes with their black fingers –

KARMA. Sylvia, Sylvia. You've been so brave. Yes you have. You've climbed mountains, forded rivers, slept in yurts, drank yak-butter tea. You've tried everything. Done everything. I'm not saying this to patronise you. I don't patronise. I'm amazed at your openness… your guts…

SYLVIA. Stop bullshitting me, Karma!

NIMA *enters. He walks up to* SYLVIA *and takes off his sunglasses, looking directly into her eyes.*

SYLVIA *gasps and puts both hands on her face, as if seeing her own reflection truly for the first time.*

SYLVIA *faints.*

KARMA *picks* SYLVIA *up and carries her off the stage.*

NIMA *hands* BUNNY *her camera.*

Scene Thirteen

2004.

Mountain in Shangri-La.

Eighteen-year-old BUNNY *takes photos wth her Nikon SLR camera. She looks different in her mountaineering gear.*

Enter NELSON.

BUNNY (*surprised*). Hey!

NELSON (*doesn't recognise her*). Hi.

BUNNY. I met you at the hostel…

NELSON. Shaman Lodge – Bunny Mu!

BUNNY *nods.*

I'm so glad to see you. I went back to the hostel.

BUNNY. We had to sell it.

NELSON. Don't blame you. Shangri-La's become such a dump. Phoney. Tacky. Overrun by Chinese. Every second shop selling souvenirs. I'd run for the hills too. So you've taken up mountaineering?

BUNNY. I've always loved mountains. (*Beat.*) I'm a professional photographer now. I take photos and turn them into postcards.

BUNNY *takes out some postcards and shows them to* NELSON.

NELSON. You must know how good these are.

BUNNY. I climb higher than any other photographer. (*Beat.*) I sent you some postcards.

NELSON. I never got them. Father must have – I've been working in New York. I would definitely have answered. Did you want to sue that Irish photographer –

BUNNY. I asked if you could introduce me to photographers or magazines in Hong Kong. (*Beat.*) I need to get out of here.

NELSON. Let me have a think – (*Beat*.) Can you really earn a
living through photography?

BUNNY (*beat*). I do some guiding too – trekking,
mountaineering. Though it's tough. There's a Tibetan mafia
controlling... Anyway. I live with my maternal uncle – look
after his kids.

NELSON. Your brother?

BUNNY. He went to Shenzhen. To the factories.

NELSON. And your dad? Is he better?

BUNNY. He's dead.

NELSON. I'm so sorry.

   Pause.

   I'm starting a travel business. A sustainable travel company.

BUNNY. A what?

NELSON. I just couldn't get your dad's story out of my mind.
How callously he was used for *copy*, with total disregard for
his worth as a human being... I kept on wondering what I
could *do*. Then I found the solution, Bunny! In South Africa!
I'm so impressed with what they've done there – working
with tribal peoples, preserving the amazing wildlife... Look,
I have a flag, a logo, everything.

   NELSON *takes out the 'Authentic China' flag.*

   I could use a good mountaineering guide.

BUNNY. I need to get out.

NELSON. We practise sustainable tourism. Ethical tourism. We
don't make our tour guides earn their keep from
commissions and tips. We're the only travelling company in
China to pay regular salaries.

BUNNY. I'm saving up / to get out –

NELSON. You need a day job. I can offer you a most
meaningful one, in the midst of spectacular scenery, and the

chance to make very good contacts. Our clients include Kofi Annan and Robert De Niro.

BUNNY. Who?

NELSON. Do you know Michael Yamamoto?

BUNNY. I've seen his photos in the *National Geographic*.

NELSON. He leads the Silk Road photo tour for us. Think of the contacts.

BUNNY. I don't ever want to slave for tourists again.

NELSON. But I'm doing this for people like you. People damaged by irresponsible tourism. We're talking about a new paradigm here, Bunny, meaningful contact between cultures, not just consuming landscapes or seeking thrills. I believe in relationships, not transactions –

BUNNY. I don't want to be stuck here, guiding tourists along these trekking paths forever. I've so *had* it with Shangri-La.

NELSON. I know you've seen mass tourism ruining your hometown. We can reverse the trend! It doesn't have to be like this.

BUNNY. Am I the only one not allowed to travel the world – just because I happen to be Naxi and a girl?

Pause.

NELSON. We're just pioneering a trek up Mount Changbai, on the China–North Korean border. How does that sound?

Pause.

BUNNY *nods.*

NELSON *holds out his hand. They shake hands.*

Bunny, I think this is the beginning of a beautiful friendship.

Scene Fourteen

BUNNY *and* SYLVIA *enter with cameras. They squat walk, as if keeping out of sight behind tall grass.*

SYLVIA. These must be the rocks where they leave out the corpses.

BUNNY. It's snowing.

SYLVIA (*holds out her hand*). No.

BUNNY. It might get too slippery.

SYLVIA. You've never lost a client.

BUNNY. Because I pay attention to signs!

SYLVIA. Think of Nelson's face when he gets the ten million.

BUNNY. Respect the mountain!

SYLVIA. I'm the client. You have to respect me.

BUNNY. I can't do this.

SYLVIA. You scared?

BUNNY. What if the relatives are there?

SYLVIA. Karma says even the family leaves.

BUNNY. Maybe they wait, lower, on the mountain.

SYLVIA. When the spirit departs, there is only an empty shell. Emptiness. We're not in a zombie movie. They're not going to come alive and eat you, Bunny.

BUNNY. Why you do this? What you see in Living Buddha's eyes?

Pause.

SYLVIA. Myself. Decrepit. White hair, wasting flesh, sans teeth, sans eyes, sans taste, sans everything.

BUNNY. It is omen! Stop!

SYLVIA. No. I'm going. I'm going and I'm taking pictures of vulture fodder. Because photographing the dead is the strongest proof that I live.

SYLVIA *raises herself cautiously, peers through her camera lenses as if checking that the coast is clear. She straightens up.*

Come on.

SYLVIA *grabs* BUNNY *and steers her forward. They stop. They both look to where the vultures cluster around the corpses.*

BUNNY*'s legs give way and she needs to use her tripod to support herself.*

SYLVIA *looks on, utterly impassive. She puts down her camera. She is immobile.*

BUNNY *starts photographing the sky, snapping convulsively. Suddenly she stops. She sets up her tripod. She deliberates. She changes the position of the camera. She steps back, very steady now. She presses the remote control.*

Scene Fifteen

A hotel.

A banner with 'UNESCO Conference on Endangered Peoples'.

KARMA and NELSON stand across a desk from each other.

KARMA. I know we've had our differences, but all in all. It's been a long and fruitful collaboration. I certainly hope you can stay on as a consultant.

NELSON. You're trying to force me out of my own company?

KARMA. Nelson, Nelson. Two weeks ago, you were broke. CEO of a failed start-up with no cash flow and a doomed business plan. Now you're a winner. What a story. Social entrepreneur, profit and conscience – you'd be written up in *Fortune*. *Time Magazine*. *GQ*.

NELSON. I am not giving up my company.

KARMA. Your company? I take it they didn't teach Marxist-Leninist economic theory in Harvard Business School.

NELSON. Who had the idea? Who had the vision? –

KARMA. Who recruited guides, who taught them English from old BBC tapes 'Peter and Jane went to the farm today'? Who begged them to tuck in their shirts, aim into the urinal / when peeing –

NELSON. Who researched best practises, who went to South Africa to study conservation efforts, who tracked sustainable safaris –

KARMA. Conservation? Is this how you see us? Dodo tourism.

NELSON. No one's calling you a dodo. The point is, the point is –

KARMA. Yes.

NELSON. The point is – I took the risks. I gave up a very lucrative job to make life better / for your communities –

KARMA. You took the risks. You. I went from village to traumatised village, still reeling from forcible 'liberation', pleading with them to open their doors to you, 'Yes yes it's technically a Chinese company but he's from Hong Kong, he's not one of them, he wants to help', I *vouched* for you, Nelson.

Pause.

(*Quietly.*) I went from village to village, and like a miracle, as if history hadn't happened, a holy village arose from the past – and I offered it to you. And you wouldn't make me a partner, wouldn't take on a Tibetan / as business partner.

NELSON. Oh no you don't. I'm no racist. I don't have to defend my record. I have stuck my neck out, okay. I've employed political radicals, even known independence sympathisers. The number of my guides that end up in jail – a roll of honour. I didn't make you partner because you're a liar and a swindler.

KARMA (*rips down 'Endangered Peoples' banner*). You like your minorities like your pandas – picturesque, endangered, helpless. I refuse to be a panda. I refuse to go extinct. I want to live, to live well, to live like them, and if I have to –

NELSON. Break a few taboos?

KARMA. Taboos. Yes. We have smashed idols. We have burnt scriptures. We have beaten monks. We have denounced our mothers and fathers. But who made us cross those lines in the first place? Whose tank? Whose soldiers? Look at what you Chinese have made of us. Clowns, pimps, whores.

NELSON. This is just – I refuse to engage – I've slaved to give minorities an honourable way of making a living. I've nurtured them, empowered them – look at Bunny, how's she blossomed –

NIMA *enters with a large DHL courier envelope.*

So here it is. Your blood money.

NELSON *opens the document and reads it.*

There's nothing in here about buying me out! It's just a straight investment proposal –

KARMA. You're right. But here's my addendum.

KARMA *takes out another piece of paper.*

Sign it.

NELSON *scans it.*

NELSON. Get out! What cheek!

KARMA. Oh, you are signing it.

NELSON. What possible reason do I have to sign over my company to you?

KARMA. What if people found out your guide took a client to watch a sky burial, Mr Ethical Tourism?

NELSON. You're just a subcontractor. You are not Authentic China. I'll disown you. Publicly. Something I should have done a long time ago.

KARMA. Bunny took Sylvia Bass to the sky burial.

Long pause.

NELSON *is utterly devastated.*

KARMA *pushes the contract and pen over to* NELSON.

NELSON *signs.*

Scene Sixteen

2016.

Artist talk at a gallery in New York City.

BUNNY *is alone on stage, dressed in Naxi dress. She looks out at the audience.*

BUNNY. Then a vulture flew into the frame of my photo. And through the viewfinder I saw its feathers, golden in the sunlight, the arc of its flight. And suddenly a stillness came over the world. Mountain above, lake below. Heaven above, earth below. I saw how the mountains cradled the dead; how the mountains contained death, and I saw that death was a part of life; that to be truly alive you must also connect to death, and that there was no horror. Just emptiness. Peace.

Applause.

NELSON *enters and sits in the audience.*

NELSON (*quietly*). Bullshit.

BUNNY. Thank you. Thank you. Are there any questions? Yes?

Listens.

I use wide-angle lens, with the corpse in one tiny corner, covered by vulture wings. I am not voyeuristic.

Listens.

My photos do not show Tibetans as savage and barbaric. I think it is good that our bodies go back to nature. I think here, too, in the West, it is the same. The body goes into the ground, and is eaten by worms. The lady in white, please.

Listens.

In general it is good to respect taboos. Taboos around death protect us. But sometimes – 'when you see the Buddha, kill the Buddha.'

NELSON *puts up his hand.*

The gentleman over there... no, sorry sir, not you. The one in the North Face jacket.

NELSON. I was blown away by the the beauty of your photographs. But I was also repulsed. Because you've abused beauty to make us complicit in your betrayal.

BUNNY. I did not betray –

NELSON. You had a duty and a responsibility to respect the peoples you encountered, not sell them and their taboos down the river for forty pieces of silver. Or are you seriously claiming that you went up the mountain with your Western clients to *enlighten* them? (*In Chinese.*) You of all people. Your father was driven mad by a taboo-breaking Western photographer.

BUNNY (*in Chinese*). No. He was not driven mad by a western photographer. I took the photo. I photographed my father performing the secret rites.

NELSON *gets up and leaves.*

Nelson!

The lights change.

*Someone throws a bouquet on to the stage (the bouquet that
features in Scene One).* BUNNY *mechanically picks it up
and acknowledges the applause.*

The sound of champagne glasses clinking.

NELSON *enters the stage, champagne glass in hand, but
stays on the sidelines.*

BUNNY *spots him and rushes towards him, but is accosted
by* SYLVIA.

SYLVIA. Bunny! Look at you!

BUNNY. Mrs Bass.

SYLVIA. Ms Davenport. I'm using my maiden name. But
Sylvia to you, always. I'm so proud of what you've
accomplished. That was such an eye-opening trip for all of us.

BUNNY. Thank you.

SYLVIA. I'm your secret admirer. I'm the anonymous buyer
who snapped up all your photos.

BUNNY. Oh. It was you.

Pause. NELSON *approaches them.*

You know Nelson Wong.

SYLVIA. What's wrong, hun?

BUNNY. Nelson is the founder of 'Authentic China'.

SYLVIA *briefly glances at* NELSON.

SYLVIA. I sold it.

NELSON. Of course.

SYLVIA. I have my own company now. 'Eco-Funerals.'
Eco-weddings have really taken off, but when it comes to
funerals – slaves to tradition, all of us! And I thought – what
if you could choose a funeral as individual as your life? Own
your funeral, own your death! Your photos are such a good
compliment.

NELSON. Congratulations. You have certainly spotted a gap in the market.

SYLVIA. Bunny, you've got to meet my friend! A curator at the Guggenheim – ah there he is.

SYLVIA takes BUNNY by the arm and tries to steer her away from NELSON.

BUNNY. Later, Ms Davenport.

SYLVIA. The man's a curator at the Guggenheim.

BUNNY. Later.

SYLVIA stares in amazement at BUNNY.

Shrugs.

SYLVIA. Well, you let me know when you change your mind, hun.

SYLVIA exits.

Pause.

NELSON. Don't let me stand in your way.

BUNNY. Nelson.

NELSON. The goal's in sight. Reach out and grab it. Don't turn sentimental now.

BUNNY. Nelson.

NELSON. It's the fucking Guggenheim.

BUNNY. Fuck the Guggenheim.

NELSON. Isn't that what you've been aiming for all along? You in your pretty Naxi dress – you always hated dresses! – milking this whole exotic-female thing for all its worth. If it wasn't for that dress, you wouldn't be standing here now.

BUNNY. Are you jealous?

NELSON. You have no right to call yourself Naxi –

BUNNY. Who do you think you are, telling us how to live our lives? How dare you!

Pause.

NELSON. How could you?

BUNNY. Your life's work was at stake.

NELSON. You've made a travesty of my life's work. My closest associate – a taboo-breaker twice over –

BUNNY. What are taboos but lines drawn in the sand? (*Beat.*) I used to think I'd ruined everything by taking that photo. But my dad was unhinged already – volatile, violent. And it was a good photo. No. A great photo. You said it too. It showed him at his best. As I'd never known him, as I want to remember him. And because of that photo, I was spared my mother's fate – used up and dead by age thirty.

NELSON. I started 'Authentic China' precisely to save you from that kind of life –

BUNNY. 'Sustainable tourism' is just another top-down solution.

NELSON. How can you say that?

BUNNY. Hand on heart. Did you really believe all that crap?

NELSON. So I've built my life on a lie? Is that what you're saying?

BUNNY. I don't know, Nelson. You need to find that out for yourself.

BUNNY *turns away to leave.*

NELSON. Going to the Guggenheim?

BUNNY. I'm going to climb a mountain.

The End.

A Nick Hern Book

Shangri-La first published in Great Britain in 2016 as a paperback original by Nick Hern Books Limited, The Glasshouse, 49a Goldhawk Road, London W12 8QP, in association with Matthew Schmolle, the Finborough Theatre, and Yellow Earth Theatre

Shangri-La copyright © 2016 Amy Ng

Amy Ng has asserted her moral right to be identified as the author of this work

Cover image: Sofi Lee Henson and Rebecca Pitt

Designed and typeset by Nick Hern Books, London
Printed in Great Britain by Mimeo Ltd, Huntingdon, Cambridgeshire PE29 6XX

A CIP catalogue record for this book is available from the British Library

ISBN   978 1 84842 610 8